OUR BODIES

THE BRAIN AND NERVOUS SYSTEM

Steve Parker

Raintree

Chicago, Illinois

Titles in the series:
The Brain and Nervous System • Digestion
The Heart, Lungs, and Blood • Reproduction
The Senses • The Skeleton and Muscles

Library of Congress Cataloging-in-Publication Data:

Parker, Steve.
  The brain and nervous system / Steve Parker.
      v. cm. -- (Our bodies)
Includes bibliographical references and index.
Contents: Parts of the nervous system -- Nerve cells -- Nerve signals --
Nerve network -- The spinal cord.
  ISBN 0-7398-6619-2 (lib. bdg. : hc)
  1. Nervous system--Juvenile literature. 2. Brain--Juvenile
literature. [1. Nervous system. 2. Brain.] I. Title. II. Series.
  QP361.5.P35 2004
  612.8--dc21

                          2003010548

08 07 06 05 04
10 9 8 7 6 5 4 3 2 1

Acknowledgments
The publishers would like to thank the following for permission to reproduce photographs:
Front cover (main image), p. 5 ImageState; front cover (inset), pp. 11 (bottom) 13 (bottom), 15 (top, bottom), 17, 23, 23, 26, 27, 31, 35, 43, 45 Science Photo Library: front cover (inset) (Catherine Pouedras/ Eurelios), 11 bottom (Tek Image), 13 bottom (Samuel Ashfield), 15 top (BSIP, James Cavallini), 15 bottom (Volker Steger), 17 (Dr John Zajicek), 23 (Mehau Kulyk), 24 (Steve Grand), 26 (TRL Ltd), 27 (GCa-CNRI), 31 (Catherine Pouedras/Eurelios), 35 (Innerspace Imaging), 43 (Simon Fraser), 45 (BSIP, Laurent/Lae. Hop Amer); pp. 1, 13 (top) 20 (bottom), 33, 41 Digital Vision; pp. 4, 38 Corbis: p.4 (LWA-JDC), p. 38 (David Turnley); pp. 7, 37, FLPA: p. 7 (Tony Wharton), p. 37 (Martin B. Withers); p. 9 (top) Ardea (Hayden Oake); p. 29 (bottom) Corbis Digital Stock; p. 36 Getty Images (Taxi); pp. 16, 21(bottom), 29 (top), 42 Topham Picturepoint/ImageWorks;. p. 19 (top) Robert Harding Picture Library (Sharp Shooters).

CONTENTS

INTRODUCTION

Changing views

Long ago, people believed that feelings and emotions came from different parts of the body. They thought that bravery and love were based in the heart, with fear in the stomach and anger in the liver. Today we know that all these emotions and feelings happen in the **brain.** The brain is also the source of all our ideas, wishes, wants, and memories—in fact, everything to do with thinking. It is the site of what we call "the mind."

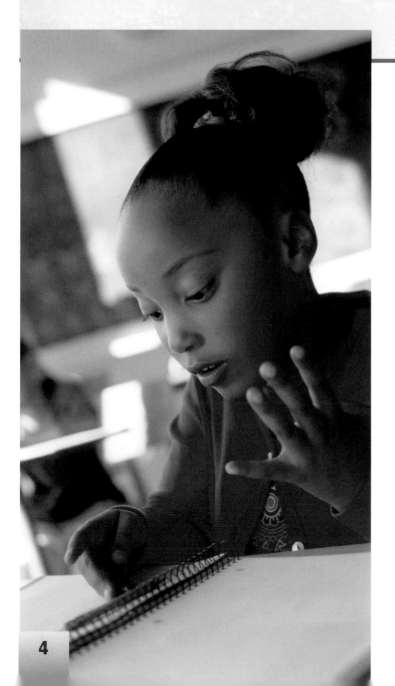

Messages in

Like a supercomputer in the middle of a vast computer network, the brain is the control center for the body. It receives millions of messages every second, information about what is happening outside the body, detected by the eyes, ears, and other senses is carried to the brain. The brain also monitors conditions inside the body, such as the heart's beating, digestion in the stomach, and the body's temperature.

We cannot see the brain working. But we can see when people are deep in thought and concentration from their facial expressions and precise actions.

In high-speed action, like skiing, the brain makes many decisions every second to control muscles and movements.

Messages out

Using this enormous amount of incoming information, the brain sends out messages to regulate and alter hundreds of body parts and processes. This, too, happens at the rate of millions of messages every second. In this way, the brain makes sure that all parts of the body work together in a coordinated way. In particular, the brain controls the muscles that make the body move.

Links to the body

Messages to and from the brain travel along **nerves.** These are like the bundles of electrical wires and optical fibers used for computer networks and the Internet. The messages themselves are in the form of tiny pulses or bursts of electricity. These are called nerve impulses or nerve signals. The nerve network spreads out through the body, with branches reaching every part, carrying information back and forth. The brain and all of the nerves combined are known as the body's nervous system.

PARTS OF THE NERVOUS SYSTEM

A multipart system

The body's nervous system is really three systems in one. First is the **brain** itself, and its main link with the body, the **spinal cord,** which passes down the body inside the back. These two parts make up the **central nervous system.** Second is the network of **nerves** that branch out from the brain and spinal cord and spread into all parts of the body. This network is known as the **peripheral nervous system.** ("Peripheral" means "away from the center" or "toward the outside.")

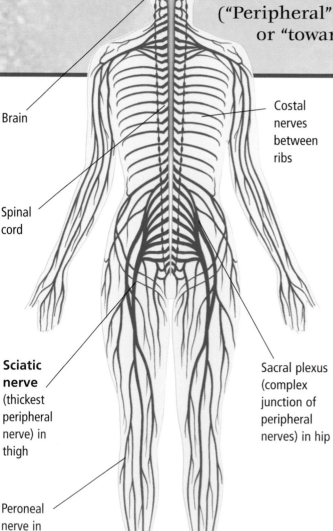

Brain

Costal nerves between ribs

Spinal cord

Sciatic nerve (thickest peripheral nerve) in thigh

Sacral plexus (complex junction of peripheral nerves) in hip

Peroneal nerve in calf

Running on auto

Third is the **autonomic nervous system.** This works like the body's "autopilot." It continually checks and monitors what is happening inside the body. This system makes alterations and adjustments to keep conditions inside the body constant and to control vital bodily processes like breathing and heart rate. It is described on pages 20–21.

The nervous system's main structural parts are the brain and spinal cord of the central nervous system, and the bodywide network of peripheral nerves (in green).

Protecting the system

The brain is soft and delicate. It is well protected inside the dome-shaped part of the skull called the **cranium.** This is made of hard bone and shields the brain from knocks and bumps. The spinal cord is also well protected from knocks, twists, and kinks. It is in a tunnel within the row of bones called **vertebrae** that make up the spine (spinal column or backbone).

Try this!

Tap your head gently. (Hopefully it does not sound hollow.) Hear and feel the hard skull bone just under the skin. This is the body's own "hard hat" to protect the delicate brain inside.

ANIMAL VERSUS HUMAN

Like jellyfish, starfish do not have real brains. They have a ring of nerves around their central part, where the arms join together. Starfish are amazingly numerous, swarming by the millions in every ocean. So big brains are not essential for the success of the species.

The main nerve

The **spinal cord** is the link between body and **brain.** It is about 17 inches (45 centimeters) long and as wide as a little finger. It is housed in a tunnel within the **vertebrae,** or backbones, of the spinal column. The spinal cord's upper end merges with the base of the brain. Its lower end, at about waist level, branches into separate **nerves** that run down the remainder of the spinal column.

Spinal cord

Left spinal nerve

Right spinal nerves

Vertebra (backbone)

Spinal cord

Intervertebral disc (pad of cartilage) at joint between vertebrae

The spinal cord is inside a tunnel within the spinal column. The spinal nerves join to it at the gaps between the vertebra (backbones), where the bones are held apart slightly by cushionlike discs.

Spinal nerves

There are 31 pairs of spinal nerves that join to the spinal cord on the left and right sides. The spinal nerves branch from the cord at gaps in the joints between the vertebrae (backbones) and spread out into the body. The uppermost nerves, located in the neck, extend down the arms and hands. The middle ones send branches to the chest and abdomen. The lowest spinal nerves extend into the legs. All of these nerves carry signals back and forth between body parts and the spinal cord.

Top Tips

The upper spinal cord is at risk during a car accident. Damage can cause pain and even paralysis (inability to move) of parts of the body below the neck. A seatbelt and a properly adjusted headrest help to greatly reduce the chance of neck and spinal cord injuries from accidents.

Inside the spinal cord

A slice through the spinal cord would show an H-shaped darker area of gray matter, set within a paler area of white matter. The white matter is mainly nerve fibers carrying nerve signals up and down the cord and linking to the brain. The gray matter is largely the cell bodies of nerve **cells,** with their millions of **dendrites** (see page 11) connecting to each other.

The spinal cord contains areas of white matter (here shown pinkish) surrounding gray matter (shown here n light green). Each spinal nerve divides into two roots, which then split into smaller rootlets as they join the cord.

ANIMAL VERSUS HUMAN

An expert predator like the wild cat pounces on a victim and immediately bites down hard on the back of its neck. This cuts or breaks the prey's spinal cord, so it cannot move and soon dies.

Nerve fibers running up and down cord

White matter (nerve cell fibers)

Gray matter (nerve cell bodies)

Outer covering of spinal cord

Rear or dorsal nerve rootlets

Rear or dorsal nerve root

Front or ventral nerve rootlets

Front or ventral nerve root

Junction (ganglion) of roots

Spinal nerve into body

FRONT OF BODY

NERVE CELLS

Different shapes and sizes

Like all living things, the human body is made of billions and billions of tiny **cells** of many different kinds. Each cell has a different shape and size. Most can only be seen under a microscope—about 20,000 of them would fit inside this "o." The cells of the **nervous system** differ from most other body cells in several ways—especially in how they are linked to each other.

A typical nerve cell has many short branches, **dendrites,** and one main longer, thicker one, the axon or fiber.

Myelin sheath around axon

Axon (fiber)

Nerve cell nucleus (control center)

Dendrites

Nerve cell body

Dendrites

Axon terminals (endings)

The nerve cell

The main types of cells in the nervous system are **nerve** cells, or neurons. There are more than one billion in the brain alone. The main part, or cell body, of a nerve cell is similar in size and shape to the cell bodies of other cells. It has the usual parts, including its own control center or nucleus.

Top Tips

In some sports and activities, there is a risk of injury that might trap or pinch a nerve, especially where it passes near a joint. This can cause pain, numbness, and inability to move the body part. Protective joint guards, such as elbow shields and knee pads, help to reduce the risk.

Dendrites

A nerve cell differs from other cells in two main ways—its **dendrites** and its **axon** (fiber). Dendrites are thin, spidery branches from the main cell body. They spread out and link to other nerve cells nearby and receive nerve signals from them. A single nerve cell may have tens of thousands of dendrites receiving signals from thousands of other nerve cells.

Axons

A nerve cell also has a longer and thicker part, called the axon or nerve fiber. In many nerves this axon is covered by a layer of fatty substance known as a **myelin sheath.** At its end the axon links to other nerve cells (or muscles). It passes nerve signals to them, rather than receiving signals from them. Some nerve cells have axons three feet (one meter) in length, making them by far the longest cells in the whole body, although a single axon is far too thin to see.

BIPOLAR NERVE CELL
(cell body partway along axon)

PSEUDOUNIPOLAR NERVE CELL
(cell body on side branch of axon)

Dendrites

Cell body

Axon (fiber)

Axon terminals

MULTIPOLAR NERVE CELL
(cell body at one end of axon)

There are many different nerve cell shapes, which pass on their nerve messages in different ways.

Nerve cells are especially delicate and easily damaged by poisonous chemicals—and the damage may be permanent. Industrial workers take many precautions against touching or breathing in possibly harmful chemicals.

11

NERVE SIGNALS

The nerve impulse

A **nerve cell** is specialized to receive and send messages, in the form of nerve **impulses** or signals. A single impulse is like a tiny surge of electricity. It is received from another nerve cell by a **dendrite.** The impulse travels across the cell body and away along the **axon,** to be sent on to the dendrites of other nerve cells.

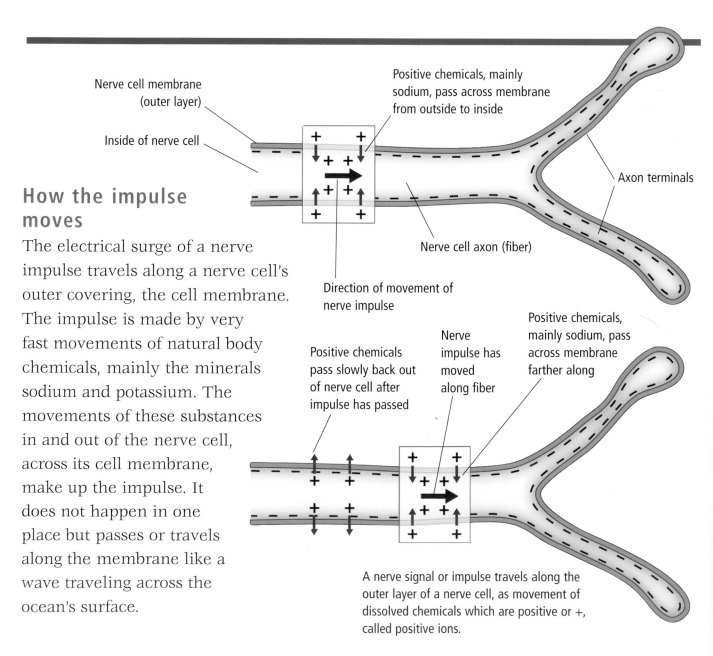

Nerve cell membrane (outer layer)

Inside of nerve cell

Positive chemicals, mainly sodium, pass across membrane from outside to inside

Axon terminals

Nerve cell axon (fiber)

Direction of movement of nerve impulse

How the impulse moves

The electrical surge of a nerve impulse travels along a nerve cell's outer covering, the cell membrane. The impulse is made by very fast movements of natural body chemicals, mainly the minerals sodium and potassium. The movements of these substances in and out of the nerve cell, across its cell membrane, make up the impulse. It does not happen in one place but passes or travels along the membrane like a wave traveling across the ocean's surface.

Positive chemicals pass slowly back out of nerve cell after impulse has passed

Nerve impulse has moved along fiber

Positive chemicals, mainly sodium, pass across membrane farther along

A nerve signal or impulse travels along the outer layer of a nerve cell, as movement of dissolved chemicals which are positive or +, called positive ions.

Jumping the gap

Where the axon of one nerve cell links to the dendrites of another, the parts do not actually touch. There are tiny gaps between them called **synaptic gaps.** A synaptic gap is about one hundred times narrower than a human hair. Even so, this is too wide for nerve impulses to "jump" across, like a spark leaping across a gap between two electrical contacts. Instead the signal passes across the gap in the form of hundreds of particles of specialized chemicals called neurotransmitters. These contact the receiving nerve cell and cause the nerve impulse to begin again.

ANIMAL VERSUS HUMAN

When snakes like cobras and mambas bite, they release poison that contains chemical substances called **neurotoxins.** These damage the nervous system, usually by stopping neurotransmitter chemicals from passing signals between nerve cells. Nerves cannot carry signals to the muscles for movement or to the lungs for breathing. So the snake's victim is paralyzed (unable to move) and may die of suffocation.

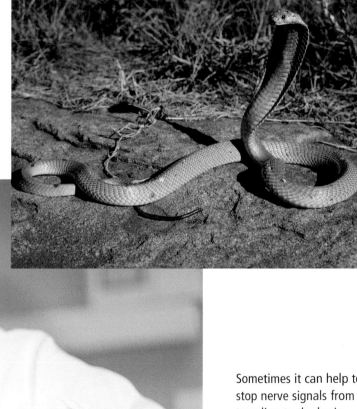

Sometimes it can help to stop nerve signals from traveling to the brain. An anesthetic does this to remove feelings, especially pain. A local anesthetic does this for only part of the body, such as the teeth during a visit to the dentist.

On the outside

Nerves have a tough, protective, gray outer layer or sheath called the **epineurium,** made of a substance called myelin. The body's thickest nerve, as wide as a thumb, is the **sciatic nerve** in the hip and upper leg. The thinnest nerves are in the muscles and are almost too narrow to see.

Inside a nerve

On the inside, the main length of a nerve consists of bundles of nerve **axons** or fibers. They look like tiny wires in a cable. Each bundle is called a **fascicle.** The **cell** bodies of these axons are mostly gathered together in lumplike parts called **ganglia,** which are located mainly along either side of the **spinal cord.**

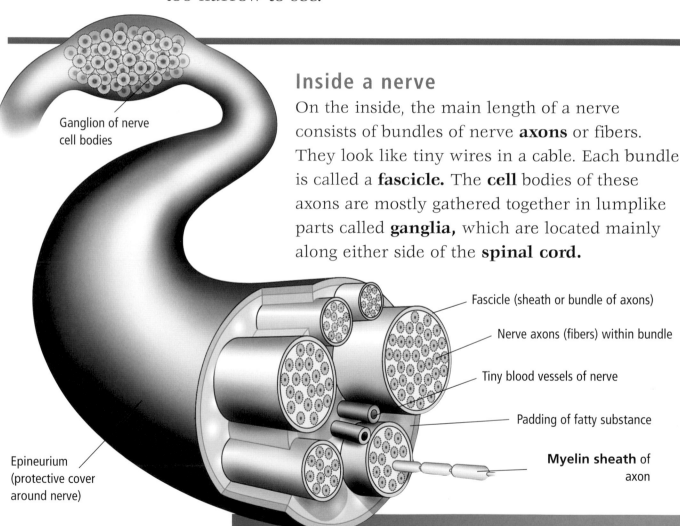

Ganglion of nerve cell bodies

Fascicle (sheath or bundle of axons)

Nerve axons (fibers) within bundle

Tiny blood vessels of nerve

Padding of fatty substance

Myelin sheath of axon

Epineurium (protective cover around nerve)

A nerve is like an electrical cable, with many nerve fibers wrapped as bundles, along with a blood supply. Fatty padding cushions these parts as the nerve bends with body movements.

Try this!

Think of a computer connected to many pieces of equipment, like a keyboard, mouse, scanner, monitor, speakers, and printer. Imagine the computer itself as a brain. Which pieces of equipment are "sensory," sending signals to the computer, and which are "motor," receiving messages from it? In this system, what are the "nerves"?

A scan of the inside of the upper leg shows how nerves like the sciatic nerve (arrowed) must withstand squashing by powerful muscles around them.

Signals through the system

A single nerve impulse has a strength of about one-tenth of one volt. (A typical flashlight battery is 15 times stronger.) The impulse is also very brief, lasting about one millisecond (one-thousandth of a second). Millions of nerve impulses pass around the nervous system every second and all are similar. The information they carry depends on how many signals there are per second and where they are going. Some go to the brain, carrying information from a sense organ like the eye. These are known as **sensory** signals. Other messages go from the brain, and most—called **motor** signals—mainly go to muscles to control the body's movements.

MICRO BODY

Under a microscope, the nerve network looks impossibly tangled. However, the individual nerve cells have very precise and accurate connections with each other.

This microscopic view shows many nerve cell bodies along the bottom with their **dendrites** and axons linking above.

NERVE DISORDERS

Nerve symptoms

When the body's peripheral **nerves** are affected, this can cause serious problems in the parts of the body they supply. These problems include numbness (inability to feel touches), weakness and trembling, spasms (uncontrolled tightening or contraction of muscles), paralysis (inability to move), and perhaps pain from the nerve itself.

Chemical damage

Some chemical substances are very harmful to nerve **cells**. They include various drugs used in nonmedical ways, especially narcotic drugs such as morphine and heroin, which interfere with the way nerve signals pass from one nerve cell to the next. Other harmful substances include alcohol, metallic chemicals like mercury, lead, and cadmium, and poisons in certain plants and fungi like mushrooms. Nerve cells are especially sensitive to such chemical damage. Many body cells can repair or replace themselves, but nerve cells are so specialized that this rarely happens. Any damage they suffer is very long-lasting.

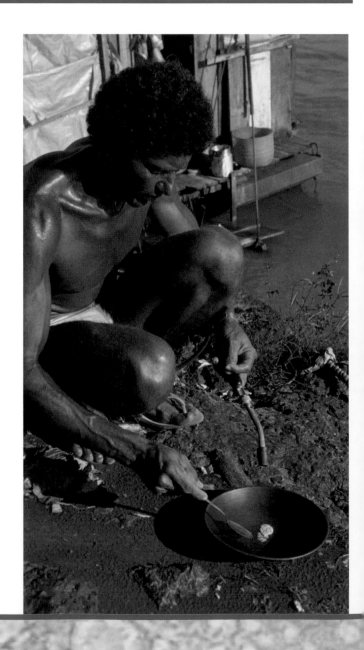

One way of obtaining tiny natural particles of gold from water is by combining them with the silvery liquid metal mercury. But mercury is very dangerous and causes damage to the nervous system.

Multiple sclerosis

In multiple sclerosis the **myelin sheaths** around nerve fibers break down. The fibers then cannot carry nerve signals properly. This may happen in several nerves, for example, those from the eyes, affecting sight, and those to various muscles, causing weakness. Usually the condition comes and goes over many years. Many people have little or no permanent disability. A few suffer greater problems and may need a wheelchair.

Motor neuron disease

Motor neuron disease affects nerve cells that carry signals to muscles. This interferes with movements, including speech, chewing and swallowing, and even breathing. The muscles gradually become weak and wasted. As with multiple sclerosis, there is no known cure.

Microbe attack

In shingles germs called *Herpes zoster* viruses multiply and attack certain nerves. This causes intense, burning pain in the nerve, and usually blisters on the skin above the nerve. The *Herpes zoster* virus also causes chicken pox, and shingles tends to occur in people who had chicken pox in the past.

MICRO BODY

Myelin sheaths work like the plastic insulation around electrical wires to speed nerve signals and keep them from leaking away. In multiple sclerosis the sheaths become damaged, hardened, and scarred, or **sclerosed.**

In multiple sclerosis nerve cells and the myelin coverings of their thin, delicate **axons** (shown here in mauve) are mistakenly attacked by the body's own defense cells (white).

REFLEX ACTIONS

No need for the brain

The **brain** controls most of the body's movements—but not all of them. In some situations, a part of the body makes a movement automatically, without the brain thinking about it or making a decision. These rapid, automatic actions are known as **reflexes.** Examples include the knee-jerk (see below), blinking when the eye's surface is touched, sneezing when the nose is irritated by dust or germs, and pulling a body part away from danger such as a sharp point or great heat.

Useful reflexes

Most reflexes are rapid reactions to help the body keep its balance and posture, or to protect itself and avoid danger, even when the brain is busy concentrating on other thoughts. The knee-jerk reflex may happen when a person stands up for a long time. Gradually the knees may sag and bend slightly. This sets off the reflex, which jerks the knee to make the leg straight and support the body again.

7 Motor signals make thigh muscle contract

6 Motor signals from cord

3 Sensory signals carry information about touch on knee

1 Stimulus – tap on knee

2 Stimulus stretches ligament under kneecap

8 Thigh muscle contraction jerks shin and foot up

4 Sensory signals to spinal cord

5 Connection (synapse) within spinal cord

In some fast "reflex" actions, such as when a goalie saves a ball, a person cannot recall making the decision to carry out the action. It all happens too rapidly and automatically.

How a reflex works

A typical reflex starts when the body senses a sudden change that could be harmful. For example, the skin of the fingers might suddenly feel great heat when the person's eyes and attention are directed elsewhere. Warning **nerve** signals flash along the nerve to the **spinal cord,** at a speed of 328 feet (100 meters) per second or more. Inside the cord, these **sensory** nerve signals pass directly to **motor** nerve **cells**. They immediately send signals out along their nerve fibers to nearby muscles, making them contract to carry out the movement. A split second later, more signals pass up the spinal cord to the brain. The brain becomes aware of what is happening, but cannot stop the reflex.

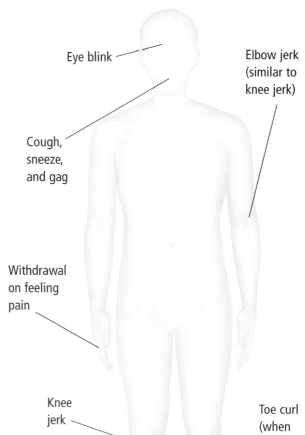

Eye blink

Elbow jerk (similar to knee jerk)

Cough, sneeze, and gag

Withdrawal on feeling pain

Knee jerk

Toe curl (when sole of foot is stroked)

The body has many types of reflexes. In withdrawal, any part that senses pain is pulled away.

Try this!

To test the knee-jerk reflex, sit on a chair with legs crossed, one knee under the crook of the other. Ask a friend to gently tap the upper leg, just below the kneecap, with a narrow item like the edge of a book. The leg "kicks" from the knee down as the reflex action makes the muscles contract.

When we are not aware

The **autonomic nervous system** is made up of various parts within the **brain, spinal cord**, and peripheral **nerves.** It works as part of the overall nervous system, but in ways we rarely realize. Most of its activities are **subconscious—** that is, they happen without our awareness. They occur automatically, without any need for us to think about them or make decisions.

Spinal cord

Right autonomic nerve trunk

Left autonomic nerve trunk

The autonomic nervous system uses many of the same parts as the other nerve systems. Two of its major parts are the autonomic nerve trunks, chains of nerves running along each side of the spinal cord.

Steady state

The autonomic nervous system deals mainly with conditions and processes inside the body. These include body temperature, heart rate, blood pressure, digestion, breathing, and making energy available for the huge variety of life processes. The autonomic system monitors all of these and more. It sends out nerve signals to adjust processes and keep conditions within the body the same, or constant, so that all body parts can work most effectively. Keeping conditions constant and stable like this, in a "steady state," is known as homeostasis.

ANIMAL VERSUS HUMAN

Antelopes graze peacefully but, if they sense danger, they race away at high speed. The autonomic nervous system makes their heart rate and breathing speed up, preparing their muscles for action in less than a second. The same happens in the human body when danger appears, but it takes a few seconds longer. It is called the "fight or flight" reaction.

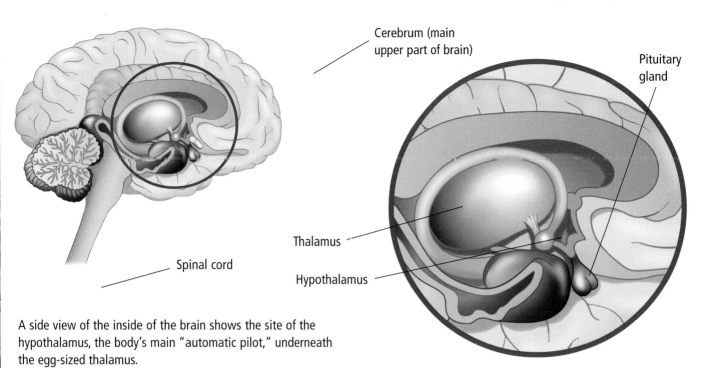

Cerebrum (main upper part of brain)

Pituitary gland

Thalamus

Hypothalamus

Spinal cord

A side view of the inside of the brain shows the site of the hypothalamus, the body's main "automatic pilot," underneath the egg-sized thalamus.

Fast and slow

The central controller of the autonomic nervous system is a small area of the brain called the hypothalamus (see pages 38–39). This part sends out two sets of nerve signals, along two sets of nerve pathways, but mostly to the same body parts. One set of nerve pathways is called **sympathetic,** the other is **parasympathetic.** Sympathetic nerve messages make body parts increase their activity and work faster. For example, heart rate quickens and breathing deepens. Parasympathetic messages do the opposite. They make the parts decrease their activity and work slower. Using this double-action control, "faster" or "slower," the autonomic nervous system keeps the body working well inside so the brain has time for more interesting thoughts.

When we become excited or frightened (or both), the hypothalamus makes many body parts speed up.

21

CRANIAL NERVES

Direct to the brain

Some of the body's **nerves** join directly to the **brain** rather than to the **spinal cord.** These are called cranial nerves and there are twelve pairs, left and right in each pair. Some are **sensory** nerves and bring signals from the main sense organs—the eyes, ears, nose, tongue—and the skin of the head. Others are **motor** nerves and carry signals to the muscles of the face, head, and neck for making movements such as chewing, swallowing, speaking, and facial expressions.

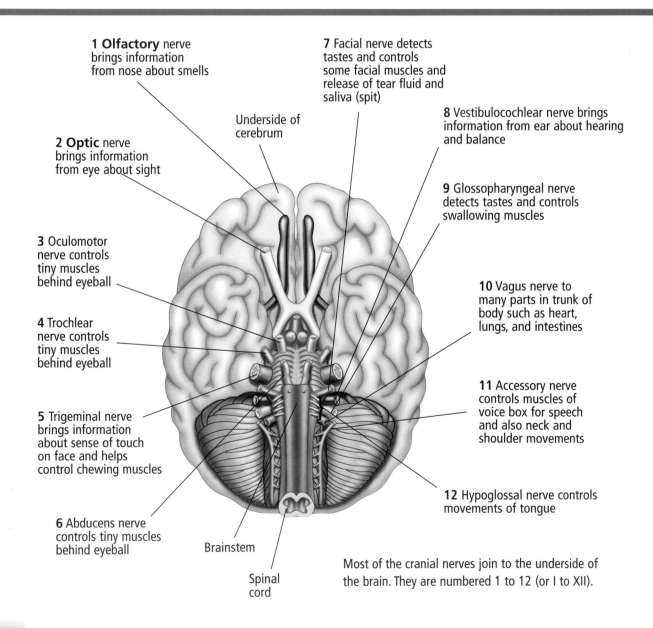

1 Olfactory nerve brings information from nose about smells

2 Optic nerve brings information from eye about sight

3 Oculomotor nerve controls tiny muscles behind eyeball

4 Trochlear nerve controls tiny muscles behind eyeball

5 Trigeminal nerve brings information about sense of touch on face and helps control chewing muscles

6 Abducens nerve controls tiny muscles behind eyeball

Underside of cerebrum

Brainstem

Spinal cord

7 Facial nerve detects tastes and controls some facial muscles and release of tear fluid and saliva (spit)

8 Vestibulocochlear nerve brings information from ear about hearing and balance

9 Glossopharyngeal nerve detects tastes and controls swallowing muscles

10 Vagus nerve to many parts in trunk of body such as heart, lungs, and intestines

11 Accessory nerve controls muscles of voice box for speech and also neck and shoulder movements

12 Hypoglossal nerve controls movements of tongue

Most of the cranial nerves join to the underside of the brain. They are numbered 1 to 12 (or I to XII).

Mixed nerves

Some cranial nerves are "mixed." This means they carry both sensory and motor signals. An example is the trigeminal nerve (cranial nerve number 5), with several branches around the side of the head. It brings sensory information to the brain about touch on the eye, eyelid, the skin of the forehead and cheek, and inside the mouth including the gums. Its motor signals go to the muscles on the side of the head that work the jaws for biting and chewing. The biggest cranial nerve is the vagus (number 10), which is also mixed. It branches down through the neck to the lungs, heart, stomach, and other parts in the trunk of the body.

Main senses

Ten pairs of cranial nerves join to the lower part of the brain, which is known as the brainstem. Two pairs link to the upper part of the brain, the cerebrum. These are the olfactory and optic nerves (cranial nerves numbers 1 and 2). They are both sensory, bringing vital information to the brain about what the nose smells and what the eyes see.

MICRO BODY

The trigeminal nerve (number 5) is one of the main cranial nerves bringing nerve signals about the sense of touch on the face. Its branches extend around the eyes and also down to the cheeks, chin, and jaws.

This combined medical scan shows the branches of several cranial nerves spreading out from the brainstem (arrowed).

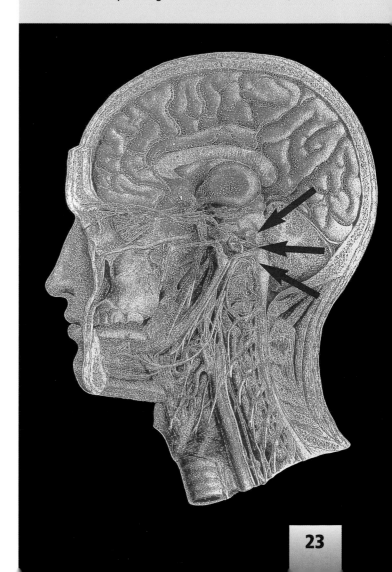

Try this!

Look at your face in a mirror. Turn your head but keep your gaze straight ahead. As your face turns to one side, your eyes swivel to the other so you keep looking forward. Three cranial nerves (numbers 3, 4, and 6) control the tiny muscles behind the eye that move the eyeball.

AROUND THE BRAIN

Three layers

The **brain** has three sheet-like layers or membranes around it, between the outside of the brain and the inside of the skull. These layers are called the dura mater (on the outside next to the skull), the arachnoid, and the pia mater (on the inside, next to the brain). Together they are known as the meninges.

The cerebrospinal fluid shows up on a scan as a dark "gap" around the outside of the brain.

Soft cushion

The arachnoid contains many blood vessels. Between it and the pia mater, there is also a layer of special liquid called cerebrospinal fluid. The meninges and fluid form a soft, cushionlike surrounding for the brain so it does not bang against the inside of the skull when the head is moved suddenly or knocked. The three meninges, and the fluid between the inner two, extend all around the brain and also downward and around the whole length of the **spinal cord.** They protect and cushion the cord, too.

Top Tips

The brain has several layers of protection—meninges and fluid, skull bone, skin of the scalp, and in many people, hair, too. However, in some situations, like construction sites, or playing certain sports, this may not be enough. A hard hat or helmet is needed to shield against knocks and bumps.

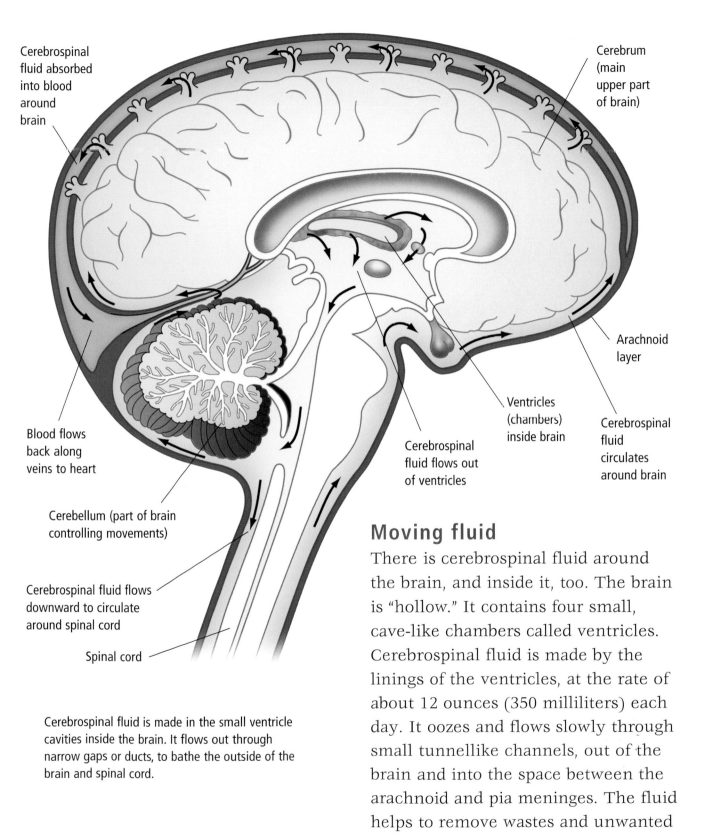

Cerebrospinal fluid absorbed into blood around brain

Cerebrum (main upper part of brain)

Blood flows back along veins to heart

Cerebellum (part of brain controlling movements)

Cerebrospinal fluid flows downward to circulate around spinal cord

Spinal cord

Arachnoid layer

Ventricles (chambers) inside brain

Cerebrospinal fluid flows out of ventricles

Cerebrospinal fluid circulates around brain

Cerebrospinal fluid is made in the small ventricle cavities inside the brain. It flows out through narrow gaps or ducts, to bathe the outside of the brain and spinal cord.

Moving fluid

There is cerebrospinal fluid around the brain, and inside it, too. The brain is "hollow." It contains four small, cave-like chambers called ventricles. Cerebrospinal fluid is made by the linings of the ventricles, at the rate of about 12 ounces (350 milliliters) each day. It oozes and flows slowly through small tunnellike channels, out of the brain and into the space between the arachnoid and pia meninges. The fluid helps to remove wastes and unwanted substances and is absorbed, at the same rate it is made, by the blood vessels in the arachnoid layer.

BRAIN AND NERVE INJURIES

Causes of injury

The **brain** and **spinal cord** are so vital that if they are injured the person's life may be in danger. Knocks, blows, or wounds to the head, neck, chest, and back are the most common causes of brain or spinal cord injury. They occur most often in car accidents and falls. Other causes include bullets from guns, knife wounds, collisions during sports, and diving into water that is too shallow.

Modern cars have airbags that inflate in an emergency to prevent the head from smashing forward and damaging the face and brain.

Effects of injury

Sometimes a brain or spinal cord injury is minor. However, almost any kind of damage to the nervous system takes a long time to heal, usually weeks or months. In more serious cases the person is disabled or affected for years, even for life. Damage to the lower spinal cord affects the lower body and legs, causing varying amounts of numbness, paralysis, and perhaps loss of control of the bladder and bowels. Damage to the upper spinal cord in the neck affects the arms as well. It may even cause problems with breathing, which can be life threatening.

Knockout

A blow to the head may cause a concussion—a brief loss of consciousness, when the person "blacks out" or is "knocked out." In some cases the person may seem to recover, apart from a sore head. But there might be underlying damage such as bleeding into or around the brain, called a hemorrhage. Anyone who is knocked out, even for a few seconds, should consult a doctor.

A horizontal brain scan through the upper part of the head shows the brain's main upper part, the cerebrum. A large area of blood (green and blue) has hemorrhaged or leaked into and over it.

Top Tips

Everyone who rides a bicycle thinks that a fall or crash will not happen—until it does. It may not be the rider's fault, but it is the rider's head and brain that are at risk. This is why it is so important to wear hard or padded bicycle helmets. In most cycling events, they must be worn as part of the rules.

THE BRAINSTEM

The "stalk" of the brain

Most of the **brain** is made of the large, bulging, wrinkled part at the top, known as the cerebrum. Below this the brain becomes narrower as it tapers downward to join the **spinal cord.** This lowest part of the brain, which is like a stalk or the trunk of a tree, is called the brainstem.

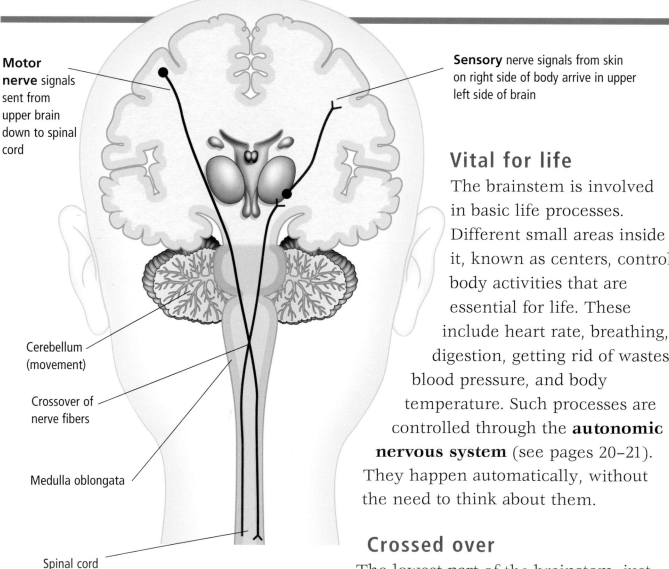

Motor nerve signals sent from upper brain down to spinal cord

Sensory nerve signals from skin on right side of body arrive in upper left side of brain

Cerebellum (movement)

Crossover of nerve fibers

Medulla oblongata

Spinal cord

Nerve fibers from the body change sides as they pass through the medulla of the lower brain.

Vital for life

The brainstem is involved in basic life processes. Different small areas inside it, known as centers, control body activities that are essential for life. These include heart rate, breathing, digestion, getting rid of wastes, blood pressure, and body temperature. Such processes are controlled through the **autonomic nervous system** (see pages 20–21). They happen automatically, without the need to think about them.

Crossed over

The lowest part of the brainstem, just above the spinal cord, is the medulla oblongata. It is slightly wider and shorter than a thumb. Thousands of nerve fibers pass through it, between the spinal cord below and the higher "thinking" parts of the brain above. However, on their way through the medulla, the nerve fibers from the left side of the spinal cord pass over to the right side. Similarly the right-side fibers cross to the left. This means the right side of the brain receives messages from, and sends message to, the left side of the body. In the same way, the brain's left side receives sensations from, and controls muscles in, the body's right side.

Nerve signals for moving the left arm to catch a ball, and feeling the ball arrive, happen in the right side of the brain.

IN THE BRAIN'S MIDDLE

Go-betweens

In the middle of the **brain** are parts called the thalamus and basal ganglia. They are between the "automatic" or "nonthinking" parts of the brain below, and the "thinking" parts above. They have various complicated tasks in the overall workings of the brain.

The middle parts of the brain have complex shapes and functions. The hippocampus is involved in memory and the caudate and lentiform nuclei are parts of the basal ganglia.

Caudate nucleus

Hippocampus

Thalamus

Medulla

Spinal cord

Lentiform nucleus

Amygdala

The thalamus

The thalamus consists of two egg-shaped parts that have **nerve** links with many other areas of the brain. It can be compared to a receptionist in a busy office. It receives nerve messages from certain parts of the brain, and sends them on, or relays them, to other parts. For example, the thalamus relays **sensory** nerve signals from the eyes, ears, and other sense organs (apart from the nose), to higher brain parts.

It also sorts out and directs **motor** nerve signals heading out to control muscles and movements. The thalamus is involved in the brain's levels of awareness—from being fully awake and alert, to being relaxed and rested, to feeling tired and drowsy, to falling into a deep sleep.

Familiar movements

Around the thalamus are several brain parts that make up the basal ganglia. Early in life a young child learns many basic movements, like chewing, swallowing, and the leg and arm actions of walking. These become so familiar and easy that we do them "almost without thinking." The basal ganglia are important in controlling and carrying out these movements.

MICRO BODY

In the condition known as Parkinson's disease, movements become weak and trembling because of problems in the basal ganglia.

In Parkinson's disease the microscopic nerve cells of the substantia nigra, which is in the lowermost area of the basal ganglia, fail to work properly due to a lack of neurotransmitter chemicals.

THE CEREBELLUM AND MOVEMENT

Parietal lobe
of cerebrum

Frontal lobe
of cerebrum

Occipital
lobe of
cerebrum

Cerebellum

Spinal cord

Brainstem

Temporal
lobe of
cerebrum

The cerebellum is the smaller, wrinkled part at
the lower rear underside of the brain.

Muscle control

When we decide to make a movement, the **nerve** signals that represent this thought are in the uppermost domed part of the **brain,** the cerebrum. This part sends more signals along nerve fibers, through the middle of the brain, and down to the round, wrinkled part at the lower rear. This is called the cerebellum and it makes up about one-tenth of the brain's total size. The cerebellum's main task is to control the individual muscles that move the body.

Smoother movements

Even a simple movement like raising the arm uses more than 20 muscles. The nerve signals from the cerebrum to the cerebellum are not very detailed—for example, giving the general instruction, "lift the arm." The cerebellum then fills in the details and sends out signals to the individual muscles that are needed for that movement. It controls the muscles in groups or teams, so that they work together in a precise and coordinated way. This means we can learn to make our movements smoother and more skilled—whether it's lifting heavy weights, or adding tiny details to a drawing.

Feedback

As a movement happens, the cerebellum receives incoming nerve messages from movement sensors in the muscles and joints. These tell it how fast the movement is occurring and how far the body parts have changed position, many times each second. Using this feedback the cerebellum can then adjust its outgoing signals to the muscles, controlling how much they pull or contract, and how fast they work, so the action happens in a smooth and coordinated way.

Try this!

With pen and paper, close your eyes, then write a common saying like "The cat sat on the mat." Now look. How neat are the words? The cerebellum plays a large part in familiar, practiced, delicate actions like writing. However, it is helpful to see the words as they are written. Then we can make adjustments like keeping the line straight and the letters the same size.

This windsurfer is relying greatly on the brain's cerebellum to control the details of muscle movements, while the thinking parts of the brain concentrate on more major decisions.

THE CORTEX AND THINKING

Gray matter

The biggest, most bulging, most wrinkled part of the **brain** is the cerebrum. It forms more than nine-tenths of the brain's total volume, and it covers the other, smaller parts beneath it. The cerebrum has an outer gray layer known as the cerebral cortex. This is similar to the "gray matter" inside the **spinal cord** and covering the cerebellum. It is made of billions and billions of **nerve cell** bodies, with trillions and trillions of **dendrite** connections. Under the gray cerebral cortex are layers of much paler "white matter." These are mainly nerve fibers linking the nerve cells of the cortex with other parts of the brain below.

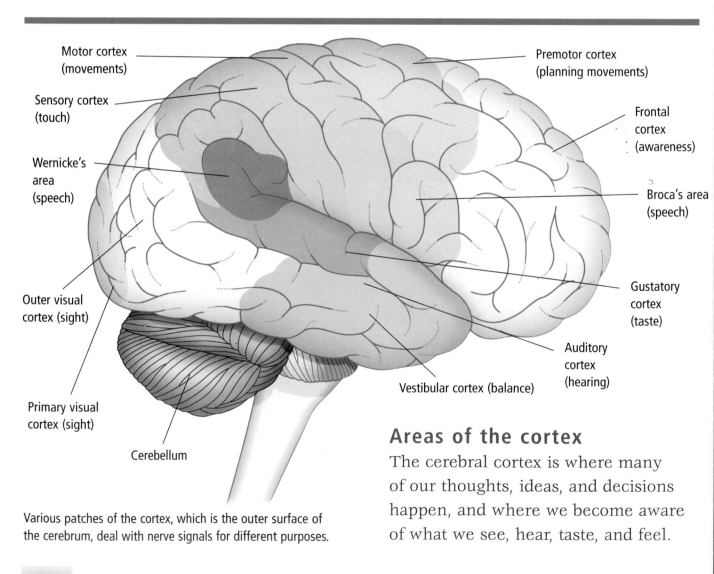

Motor cortex (movements)

Sensory cortex (touch)

Wernicke's area (speech)

Outer visual cortex (sight)

Primary visual cortex (sight)

Cerebellum

Premotor cortex (planning movements)

Frontal cortex (awareness)

Broca's area (speech)

Gustatory cortex (taste)

Auditory cortex (hearing)

Vestibular cortex (balance)

Various patches of the cortex, which is the outer surface of the cerebrum, deal with nerve signals for different purposes.

Areas of the cortex

The cerebral cortex is where many of our thoughts, ideas, and decisions happen, and where we become aware of what we see, hear, taste, and feel.

It looks much the same all over. But areas or patches of it are specialized for dealing with nerve signals coming from, or going to, different body parts. For example, around the lower rear of the cerebrum is the visual cortex. This area receives and sorts nerve messages from the eyes and compares them with information already in the brain about shapes, colors, and patterns. This is how we can make sense of what we see and recognize scenes and objects. There are similar areas of cortex for hearing, touch, taste, balance, understanding speech and writing, speaking words, and planning and making movements (**motor** cortex).

Try this!

Sit in front of a sheet of paper, and draw a dot somewhere on it. Close your eyes, and after a few seconds, try to touch the dot with your finger. You can remember a picture of the paper in your "mind's eye," and move your hand to reach it (or very near). This type of memory, called visual-spatial awareness, is based in the frontal cortex (see opposite).

MICRO BODY

The cortex of the cerebrum contains billions of nerve cell bodies, with their dendrites linking to each other to form an incredibly complex network. This is where most general thinking or mental processes happen.

The nerve cell bodies in the cortex are shown as dark spots, and the dendrites as thin lines, in this micro view.

Hemispheres

The main bulging part of the **brain,** the cerebrum, has a rounded shape like a wrinkled soccer ball. But there is an extra-deep groove from front to back that almost divides the cerebrum into two halves. These halves are called the left and right cerebral hemispheres. At the base of the split is a connecting strap between the two halves, called the corpus callosum. This contains more than 100 million **nerve** fibers. They carry nerve signals between the left and right halves, so information can be sent back and forth.

When a person plays music with great feeling, the right side of the brain tends to be in charge, or dominant, over the left side.

Two halves make a whole

The two cerebral hemispheres appear similar. But they have slightly different jobs. Usually, one is "dominant," and takes charge over the other. For example, areas called speech centers in each hemisphere deal with the process of choosing words, putting them into a sensible order, and speaking them out loud. In most people, by the age of 8–10 years, the left speech center becomes dominant and takes charge, while the right one is quiet or "dormant."

Left and right

There are other differences in the ways that the left and right sides work. In general, the left side has more to do with words and language, numbers and math, and solving problems in a step-by-step way. The right side tends to deal more with intuition or "jumping" to answers, and awareness of shapes, patterns, colors, and musical sounds. Of course, in daily life, both halves of the brain work closely together.

ANIMAL VERSUS HUMAN

About one person in ten prefers to use the left hand for holding, writing, and similar actions, while the rest prefer the right hand. Animals like chimpanzees also prefer to use one hand rather than the other, for detailed tasks. Even snails can be "left-handed" or "right-handed." Seen from above, a left-handed snail shell twists to the left (counter-clockwise) while others swirl to the right.

FEELINGS AND EMOTIONS

Where is "the mind"?

There is no single place in the **brain** that can be called "the mind" where all thoughts, ideas, and memories happen. Different parts of the brain work together in a very complicated way. This includes the way that people experience strong feelings and powerful emotions, such as fear, anger, rage, pain, pleasure, and love. Many parts of the cerebral cortex are involved in these feelings. Millions of **nerve** messages pass between, and are sent out to, other brain parts, especially the thalamus, the cerebellum, and the hypothalamus.

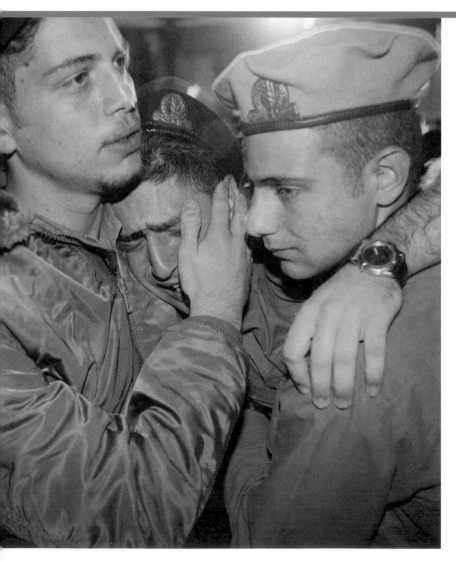

Emotions and behavior

Sometimes feelings and emotions are so strong, a person seems overwhelmed by them and unable to think clearly or sensibly. This type of behavior especially involves the hypothalamus, a small part at the lower front of the brain. It receives nerve messages from the cerebral cortex and other brain areas and sends out its own signals through the **autonomic nervous system** (see pages 20–21) to many body parts. This causes the reactions that accompany powerful emotions, like quickened heart rate, panting

Bad news can cause such powerful emotions that they take over the sensible, rational, "thinking" functions of the brain.

(fast, shallow breathing), blushing of the skin, sweaty or clammy hands and face, dry mouth, and "butterflies" or "flutterings" in the stomach and digestive system.

Hot and thirsty

The hypothalamus performs many other vital jobs. It has a "temperature center" that helps to monitor and adjust body temperature, keeping it within a very narrow range, usually 98.6 °F (37 °C). It also has a "thirst center" that checks the amount of water in the blood. This, in turn, shows the amount of water in the body. If there is too little, the hypothalamus makes us feel thirsty.

The hypothalamus is hardly larger than the tip of a little finger. Yet it has very important roles in many vital brain activities, including links with the body's second control system, the hormonal system, through the pituitary gland just below it.

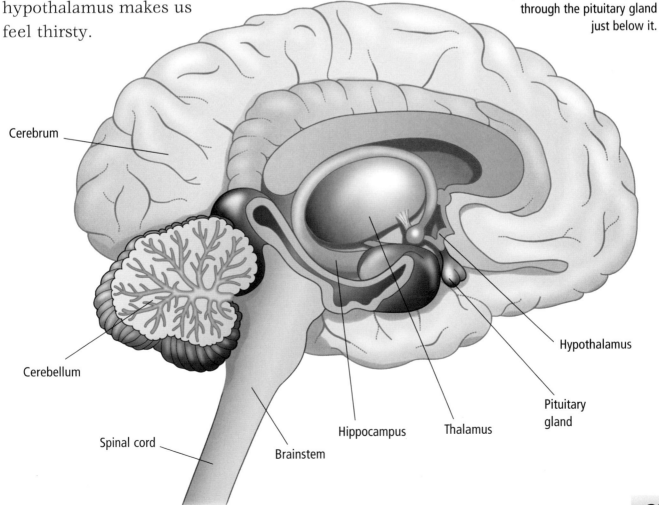

Cerebrum

Cerebellum

Spinal cord

Brainstem

Hippocampus

Thalamus

Hypothalamus

Pituitary gland

LEARNING

Learning all the time

How much will you learn today? We learn at school, but we also learn in other ways during everyday life, often without realizing it. We learn how to behave in certain situations, our likes and dislikes, and information about our family and friends. Whatever we learn is stored as memories in the **brain,** so we can recall or remember them later.

Parts involved in memory

Like other types of thinking and behaving, there does not appear to be a single place in the brain where all memories are stored. Memories are a result of many parts working together. These parts include various areas of the cerebral cortex, especially toward the front side of the brain (known as the prefrontal cortex); the thalamus; and also parts at the center of the cerebrum, the amygdala and hippocampus.

Thalamus

Basal nucleus

Corpus callosum (links two halves of cerebrum)

Hippocampus

Caudate nucleus

Amygdala

Blood supply along basilar artery

Many parts of the brain are involved in learning and memory. Damage to any one, or lack of blood supply, can cause memory difficulties.

40

Multiple memories

It is likely that different parts or sections of what seem like one memory are stored in different parts of the brain. For example, imagine the memory of an exciting event like a rollercoaster ride. What you can recall of the sounds of the ride may come from one part of the brain, while you remember the sights in another, and the memory of your bodily feelings is in yet another place. These "pieces of memories" probably exist as sets of connections or pathways for **nerve** signals between nerve **cells**.

ANIMAL VERSUS HUMAN

Legend has it that elephants have very long memories. Modern science shows that these age-old beliefs are true. The chief of the herd is an older female elephant, the matriarch. Studies show that she learns where there are fresh areas of plant growth to return to each year, and remembers waterholes for drinking. She builds up these memories over her lifetime, which may be more than 70 years.

BRAIN DISORDERS

Physical and mental

The **brain** is so important and complicated that if it goes wrong it can have many effects on the body. Some brain disorders are physical, which means they have a clear cause that can be detected by medical examination, X-rays, scans, or tests on brain chemicals like neurotransmitters. Other problems, including certain mental or behavioral disorders, have causes that are less easy to identify. But they are just as real for the sufferer. They are based in the mind and affect moods and emotions, and the way people think, talk, react, and cope with stress.

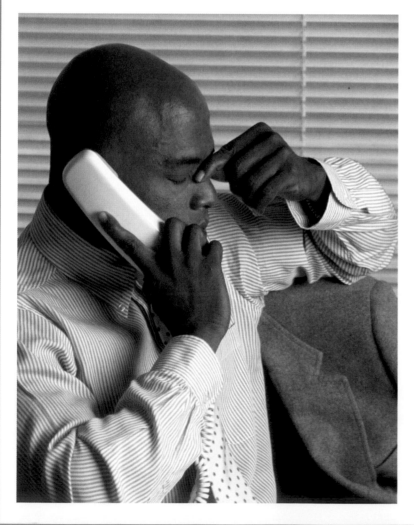

Headache

Headaches are common, yet the brain itself cannot detect pain. It does not have the right **nerve** sensors. The aching sensations usually come from around the brain, in the meninges (coverings), blood vessels, and other surrounding parts. A headache is not really a single disorder. It is a part or symptom of an underlying problem. These problems may range from tiredness and lack of sleep, to worry and stress, a bang on the head, or rarely, a growth or tumor in the brain.

Headaches often occur when a person is under stress, working long hours, and worrying about career or home life.

MICRO BODY

Alzheimer's disease is a condition in which memory begins to fade relatively early, compared to the normal process of ageing. The person may even forget family and friends.

In Alzheimer's disease, nerve cells in parts of the brain develop "tangles" as their **dendrites** and fibers are damaged and lose their connections.

Stroke and epilepsy

In a stroke, a blood vessel supplying the brain gets blocked. Blood cannot bring vital oxygen and nutrients, so parts of the brain suffer damage. Signs of a stroke include numbness and paralysis, perhaps on one side of the body, loss of speech, and possibly collapsing. In the group of conditions known as epilepsy, nerve signals pass through the brain in a random, disorganized way. This may cause jerky movements known as a seizure or convulsions, and often unconsciousness.

Brain waves

The medical EEG (electroencephalo-graph) machine detects the tiny electrical pulses of nerve signals in the brain, through pads placed on the head. It shows these signals as waves and spikes on screen or paper. EEGs help to identify various brain disorders so that treatment is more likely to be successful.

SLEEP AND DREAMS

Why do we sleep?

The sleeping **brain** is very busy, as shown by its EEG waves. But exactly what it does at this time is still partly a mystery. Recent studies show that one of the brain's tasks may be "memory-sorting." It works through its stores of memories, keeps some that are important, and throws away or forgets others.

Falling asleep

As a person falls into deep sleep, the body slows down, muscles relax, and heart rate and breathing decrease. Some processes, such as digestion and formation of urine (liquid waste) in the kidneys, also become slower. But others, like repair of wounds or damage, are faster.

REM sleep

After about one hour of deep sleep, heart rate and breathing quicken, muscles twitch, and the eyes move rapidly back and forth, even though the eyelids are closed. This is called REM (rapid eye movement) sleep, and it is when dreams occur. A person who wakes up at this time usually remembers the dream. On most nights, we pass through this first REM sleep and sink into deep sleep for another hour or so, then repeat more cycles of REM and deep sleep until morning.

Sleep varies from deep (non-REM) to shallow (REM) in stages through the night, with different EEG traces for each level (below).

Falling asleep

Waking up

A W A K E
A S L E E P

REM sleep

Shallowest sleep (stages 1 and 2)

Fairly deep sleep (stage 3)

Deep sleep gradually gets shallower towards morning

Deep sleep (stage 4)

1 Hour | 2 Hours | 3 Hours | 4 Hours | 5 Hours | 6 Hours | 7 Hours | 8 Hours

Shallow sleep (stage 1)

Shallow sleep (stage 2)

Deeper sleep (stage 3)

Deep sleep (stage 4)

REM sleep

The need for sleep

Whatever the brain does during sleep, it seems to be important, since we need enough regular sleep to stay healthy. Lack of sleep causes headaches, confusion, dizziness, poor concentration, bad temper, and loss of memory. It also makes the body more at risk from disease and infections. Sleep, like many functions of the brain and **nerves,** is complicated and fascinating. Indeed the brain is not only the control center of the body and the site of the mind—it is the only object that can find out more about itself.

Research continues into the amazingly complex workings of the brain. Even "simple" sleep is still poorly understood.

Top Tips

Some people have trouble falling asleep, or wake up too early and cannot go back to sleep. There are many pieces of advice to help them:

Adjust the bed and its covers for comfort, so it is not too warm or cold.

Think of pleasant events such as vacations.

Relax each muscle one at a time, and breathe slowly.

Put aside cares and worries until the next day, when something can be done about them.

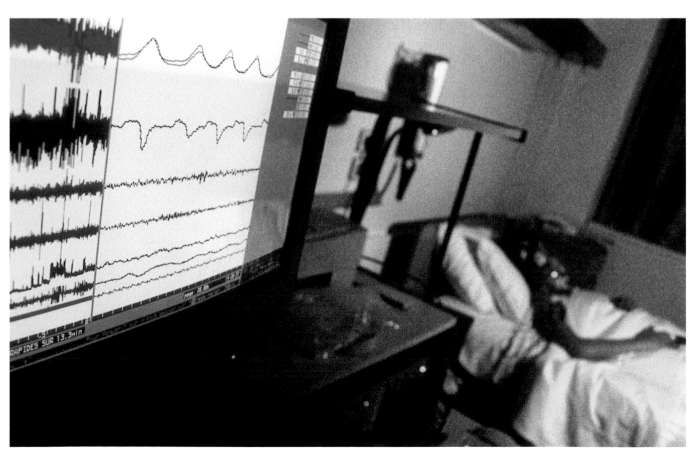

GLOSSARY

autonomic nervous system parts of the nervous system that work automatically, without us having to think about them or control them, to keep conditions inside the body constant, and to control vital bodily processes like breathing and heart rate

axon long, thin part of a nerve cell, also called a nerve fiber, that carries nerve signals away from the cell body and passes them on to other nerve cells

brain incredibly complex part of the body in the upper part of the head, made of billions of nerve cells and nerve fibers. The brain receives information from the senses, controls the body's movements, and is the site of thoughts, memories, conscious awareness, and the mind.

cell single unit or "building block" of life—the human body is made of billions of cells of many different kinds

cell body main part of a microscopic cell, usually rounded and containing tiny parts such as the cell's nucleus or control center

central nervous system brain and spinal cord

cranium "brain-case"—the curved, dome-shaped bones of the upper skull that surround and protect the brain

dendrite short, thin, branching part of a nerve cell that receives nerve signals from other nerve cells and caries them toward the cell body

epineurium covering or sheath around a nerve

fascicle group of nerve fibers within a nerve, like a bundle of wires within an electrical cable

ganglion lumplike part of a nerve that contains a group or gathering of the cell bodies from nerve cells (more than one ganglion are ganglia)

impulse tiny surge or pulse of electricity that passes along a nerve; also called a nerve signal or nerve message

motor in the body, to do with movements or motions, such as motor nerves that carry motor nerve signals to the muscles to control their movements

myelin sheath covering of certain nerve fibers (axons), made of a sheet of the fatty substance myelin wrapped around and around the fiber, like a roll of paper towels

nerve long, thin, stringlike part inside the body that carries information in the form of nerve impulses or signals

neurotoxins poisonous substances that have a harmful effect on the nerves by damaging them or stopping them from working properly

olfactory to do with the sense of smell

optic to do with the sense of sight (vision)

parasympathetic parts of the autonomic nervous system (see above) that make the body work more slowly, for example, by decreasing the rate at which the heart beats and the lungs breathe

peripheral nervous system network of nerves that branch out to all body parts from the brain and spinal cord, but not including the brain and spinal cord

reflex quick, automatic reaction by the body, to a sudden change or situation that could be harmful

sciatic nerve thickest peripheral nerve in the body, which runs from the hip down through the thigh to the knee

sclerosed hardened, stiffened, and toughened

sensory to do with body parts that detect what happens in the surroundings, such as the eyes, which sense light, and the sensory nerves, which carry sensory nerve signals to the brain

spinal cord body's main nerve, extending from the base of the brain down through the spinal column of backbones to the waist

subconscious happening in the brain, but without the mind being aware of it during conscious thoughts

sympathetic parts of the autonomic nervous system (see above) that make the body work faster, for example, by increasing the rate at which the heart beats and the lungs breathe

synaptic gap tiny gap or space in the connection or junction (synapse) between two nerve cells, where they do not quite touch but where nerve signals can pass across in chemical form

vertebrae individual bones of the backbone (spinal column or vertebral column)

FURTHER INFORMATION

BOOKS

Brynie, Faith Hickman. *The Physical Brain.* Farmington Hills, Mich: The Gale Group, 2001.

Goldsmith, Connie. *Neurological Disorders.* Farmington Hills, Mich: The Gale Group, 2001.

Hayhurst, Chris. *The Brain and Spinal Cord: Learning How We Think, Feel, and Move.* New York: Rosen, 2001.

Parker, Steve. *Body Focus: Injury, Illness, and Health–The Brain.* Chicago: Heinemann, 2003.

ORGANIZATIONS

American Epilepsy Society
342 North Main Street
West Hartford, CT 06117-2507
Phone: (860)586-7505
Fax: (860)586-7550
www.aesnet.org

Magnum
The National Migraine Awareness Group
113 South Saint Asaph Street
Suite 100
Alexandria, VA 22314
Phonc: (703) 739-9384
www.migraines.org

The National Multiple Sclerosis Society
733 Third Avenue
New York, NY 10017
Phone: (800) 344-4867
www.nationalmssociety.org

National Stroke Association
9707 E. Easter Lane
Englewood, CO 80112
Phone: (303) 649-9299
Fax: (303) 649-1328
www.stroke.org

INDEX